Questions
for
Living

Dom Helder Camara

Questions
for
Living

Translated from the French
by Robert R. Barr

ORBIS BOOKS

Maryknoll, New York 10545

Second Printing, December 1987

BX
1754.3
.C3613
1987

The Catholic Foreign Mission Society of America (Maryknoll) recruits and trains people for overseas missionary service. Through Orbis Books Maryknoll aims to foster the international dialogue that is essential to mission. The books published, however, reflect the opinions of their authors and are not meant to represent the official position of the society.

First published as *Des Questions pour vivre* by Éditions du Seuil, 27, rue Jacob, Paris VIᵉ, copyright © May 1984

English translation copyright © 1987 by Orbis Books, Maryknoll, NY 10545

Manuscript editor: Mary Heffron

Photo credits:
Frank Breen, M.M.: p. 76
Steve De Mott, M.M.: p. 24
DiGenno: p. 49
Patricia Jacobsen, M.M.: p. 79
Shirley King, M.M.: p. 64
L'Osservatore Romano: p. 29
Frank Maurovich: p. 19
Robert McCahill, M.M.: p. 61
Al Scheid: p. 86
Joseph Towle, M.M.: p. 33
Vivant Univers: pp. 73, 95
Eric Wheater: pp. 9, 12, 15, 40, 43, 55, 70
Winkler: p. 98

ORBIS/ISBN 0-88344-558-1

CONTENTS

Foreword by José de Broucker   vii

Preface   xi

1. You?   1

2. Your Prayer?   8

3. Your Hope?   11

4. Your God?   14

5. Do We Believe in Order to Hope?   18

6. Our Religion?   21

7. Your Brother John Paul II   26

8. Is the Church Really with You?   31

9. What About Our Own Church?   38

10. Capitalism or Communism?   42

11. Should We Turn Our Backs on Progress?   48

12. How Can We Help the Third World?   53

13. What Can We Do Here?   59

14. Can People Really Help?   63

15. What Good Is It . . . ?   67

16. Who, Me?   72

17. Youth? Are You Serious?   75

18. Concretely?   78

19. Shall We Lay Down Our Arms?   81

20. Does Nonviolence Work?   91

Conclusion   97

FOREWORD

"That's enough of a monologue. Let's have dialogue!" For over twenty years, Dom Helder Camara, preacher of justice and peace by active nonviolence, has invariably ended his talks with these words. It is his way of calling for questions and objections.

But for more than twenty years the dialogue has been cut short. By the time Dom Helder yields the floor and the mike, it is often late. The crowds that have gathered to see and hear him are large and the hands raised too numerous. Dom Helder's answers may be like a second, a third, and a fourth talk, in form as well as length! When the time is up, everyone is still hungry for answers and hates to leave.

Does Dom Helder Camara need an introduction? He tells his life story in *Les Conversions d'un évêque.* Born on February 7, 1909, in Fortaleza, Brazil, he has been, successively, secretary of the National Conference of Brazilian Bishops, auxiliary archbishop of Rio de Janeiro, and archbishop of Olinda and Recife. For over thirty years he has been the voice of the third world. His battle has been the battle for liberation from all oppression and all injustice, his testimony the testimony of active nonviolence, his faith the faith of the church of the poor.

In June 1983, under the auspices of the Catholic weekly *La Vie,* the archbishop of Olinda and Recife traveled throughout western France. His trip had been prepared over a period of several months by diocesan communications committees and various associations and movements involved in the struggle for solidarity, justice, and peace.

Rennes, La Roche-sur-Yon, Nantes, Angers, Cholet, Laval, Poitiers—each day at one of these stops Dom Helder would hold meetings with organizers and activists, with the press, and in the evenings with crowds of several thousand persons who had come to hear of ''the hope of the poor.''

The audiences would be told, ''Ask your questions in writing. Dom Helder will not be able to answer them all this evening, but he will answer them later, in writing, and *La Vie* will publish his answers.'' All together more than five hundred pieces of paper were handed in, many of them listing a number of questions.

Later, Dom Helder read the questions. Then, in order to gauge which of the questions from his French audiences would be relevant to persons everywhere and over a long time, he looked through questions that had been asked of him everywhere—the United States, Italy, Germany, Belgium. Next, returning to those five hundred pieces of paper, he tried especially to read between the lines so that he would miss neither any of the doubt, skepticism, or anxiety that might be there nor any of the eagerness to understand and to act that so often showed in those who had come to hear him. Behind the plaudits and the cheering, he recognized the grave questions that if left unanswered could so easily dampen enthusiasm once the celebration was over, and these simply had to be faced.

The questions were grouped according to subject, from those concerned with the person of Dom Helder himself—his personal religion, his church—to questions about his positions on politics, economics, pacifism, or nonviolence, and on to concrete inquiries about how individuals can actually conform their lives to all the lovely ideas about which Dom Helder speaks.

Now all that had to be done was to answer the questions! Dom Helder put his whole heart into the task, all of his sincerity, all of his faith in God and human beings. He called on all of his knowledge of important records and documentation. He invoked all of his respect for those who do not think as he does, for he does not believe he has the answers to all questions—Dom Helder has never tried to be a "guru" or to lead a "movement." Thus, more than once he tells a questioner that the problem is that person's own responsibility.

It was my task as editor of *La Vie* to publish Dom Helder's written answers to the questions put to him on his "pilgrimage" to Brittany and the Loire Valley. I saw at once that they could not simply all come out one fine day in the paper. What was needed was a book. And here is the book. It has been put together to afford room for a "living dialogue needed to get ideas moving," as Dom Helder likes to say.

The questions come from audiences that read *La Vie,* but the answers are addressed to all who, like them, in France and elsewhere, are unwilling to let the hope they carry within them for a better world be no more than a word, a generous but vain incantation, without any "hooks on reality."

JOSÉ DE BROUCKER

PREFACE

To evoke the thoughts of Dom Helder about addressing people in the industrial nations and answering their questions, the editors of La Vie *wrote the following and asked him to reply. His statement serves as an introduction to the rest of this book.*

Dom Helder, wherever you go, large crowds come to hear you. There's lots of applause. You always say the people encourage you. You encourage them too. But you leave many people hungry in those crowds.

In the spring of 1983, during your trip to Paris and the west of France under the auspices of La Vie, *more than thirty thousand people heard you in all. All were invited to ask their questions in writing. We have collected more than five hundred. Some you have answered verbally. But you have promised to answer the others in writing. The moment has come! Are you ready?*

Absolutely, and I understand that I must have the courage to listen and respond. When I was named archbishop of Olinda and Recife in the northeast of Brazil in 1964, I immediately grasped that in order to bring about a peaceful but effective change in the unjust structures that are crushing more than two-thirds of humanity—the so-called third world—we should have to complement our indispensable local work with a similar endeavor in the rich industrial countries.

Thanks to friendships struck up in Rome with the bishops of the whole world during the Second Ecumenical Council of the

Vatican, I began to visit other countries, especially the wealthy industrial countries.

From the very first I spoke to huge crowds, especially of young people. I felt a hunger and thirst for justice everywhere. So many persons burned with the desire to help create a more just and a more humane world. I was always well received. People could see that I was speaking with sincerity and that I was at least making an effort to live what I was saying with my lips.

But there was always a problem with the question period. The questions were serious, expressing both a desire for action and a feeling of impotence in the face of great human problems.

In the spring of 1983, during the "pastoral tour" I made with *La Vie* in Brittany and along the Loire, once more I listened to dozens upon dozens of questions. And once more the questions had much the same accent of uneasiness and sincerity, demand and confidence, doubt and hope, and a willingness not to be satisfied with nice words and good intentions. I am glad to have these questions from western France. I shall regard them as expressions of the loving challenges addressed to me by my brothers and sisters always and everywhere.

May the Lord help me to do my best. There is no way for me always to give a fully satisfactory answer, but I pray that each answer I do give will at least be accompanied by all my sincerity, all my desire to measure up to the trust my questioners have in me.

1

YOU?

Those who have not read your life story in your Les Conversions
d'un évêque *would like to know more about you now that they have
seen and heard you. For example, why aren't you a cardinal yet?
Have you refused, or have you never been invited? Is it a matter of
diplomacy?*

When the Holy Father, John Paul II, came to Brazil, as he
got off the plane in my city, Recife, he made me more than a
cardinal: he proclaimed me "brother of the poor and my
brother." Ah, that was wonderful!

I can never forget that I have already received the fullness of
the gifts of God. Without any merit on my part, I have received
the gift of life. In baptism I have received the gift of divine life.
In confirmation I have received the Holy Spirit and the Spirit's
seven gifts in a special manner. Now I have received the
ministerial priesthood, and with the episcopate, the fullness of
that priesthood.

Do you have a political party?

No. When I was a young priest, with the permission, in fact
at the request of my bishop, I worked for the Integralist Party

inspired by Salazar and Mussolini and for the League of Catholic Voters, which was not a party but a lobby to pressure candidates to push for a program drawn up by the church. I soon came to believe, and I still believe, that it is not a priest's place, and still less a bishop's place, to attempt to influence politics through a party. Politics is very important. I know that love and justice according to the gospel will pass from words to deeds only through political choices and commitments. Priests and bishops should encourage lay people to undertake these commitments in the parties of their choice. But I am convinced they should not undertake them themselves.

Do you have freedom of movement in Brazil? Are you free to do your work?

For ten years, Brazilian newspapers, radio, and television were prohibited from publishing or broadcasting any news whatever about me, positive or negative, or any document from me or about me. I no longer received any invitations, except those of a strictly religious nature, since it was known that the government would not be pleased. Now I am able to move freely about the country once more. I have always been able to move freely outside Brazil. The government let it be thought that I spent my time abroad attacking my native country, when actually I was only trying to help create a better world.

What are your daily activities when you aren't on the road?

Those of an old priest and an old bishop in the midst of his people. I celebrate Mass. I go to the "bishop's palace" in Manguinho. I work with the priests, sisters, and laity who are in charge of the pastoral ministry, religious education, solidarity, and human promotion in the diocese. I receive individuals, families, and groups who come to talk to me about their problems, and along with my coworkers I help them solve them. I visit the base communities. I listen to the Spirit of God speaking through the life of these communities, through their magnificent faith. Every morning I speak for a few minutes on Radio Olinda. And then there is all the work to be done and the meetings to be held with the other bishops of my region and with the National Conference of Brazilian Bishops.

Which comes first for you, being a priest or being a bishop?

The human creature can render even the lowliest tasks worthy. No work is unworthy of the hands of a human being. But there are tasks with a special meaning, especially those whose purpose is the service of others.

If God gave me the gift of birth a hundred times and entrusted to me a hundred times the kind of life I have lived, I would thank God a hundred times that I am a priest. A priest doesn't exist in a vacuum. A priest exists only to serve men and women and glorify God.

The episcopate, in conferring on me the fullness of the priesthood, invites me to serve even more. We have forgotten the meaning of ''minister'' and ''ministry.'' The priest, and especially the bishop, are ministers—servants.

Do you think just anyone can do what you do?

God gives me the conviction that all of us are instruments in God's hands. In full respect for our freedom and taking advantage of our weaknesses—I could even say especially by taking advantage of our weaknesses—God has us work miracles.

I appreciate the great distance between what I am saying and what those who hear me can see and recognize. Fortunately there is the breath of God's Spirit!

You're a celebrity. How does this make you feel? You have written the "Symphony of Two Worlds," and you conduct it nearly everywhere in the world. Now you speak of composing a ballet with Béjart. Aren't you afraid that stardom might compromise your mission to the poor?

When I hear about symphonies or ballets or books or when I'm invited to give a major address or do a TV program, I try to turn to the Lord at some moment when no one can hear our conversation, and I say, "Well, Lord, there's this book idea, or this symphony idea, and now something about a ballet. It's up to you. If it's only for my pleasure, my recreation, my visiting card, my fame, it's easy for you to have it not work. But if it can help ideas get moving that aren't Dom Helder's ideas but the ones your Spirit gives to all simple and upright persons, it's easy for you to have it work too. Just say the word!"

Let me explain. God has put music and harmony in all of us. The role of genuine music is to arouse the music within us that the rough, hard life we lead so often puts to sleep. Sometimes we even have the impression that it is dead.

God has stamped a rhythm in human beings, animals, plants, and even stones. A person walking, a bird flying, a leaf falling—everything proclaims the beginning of a dance. At the heart of the atom, in the ballet of the stars, rhythm and harmony have been sown by our Creator! Listening to music, watching dance—these are true prayers!

You mention the poor. It's not at all hard to understand why the poor smile with happiness when they see my picture in the papers or on TV or in store windows. . . .

The poor understand why, after asking the help of music and

God has put music and harmony in all of us.
The role of genuine music is to arouse the music
within us that the rough, hard life we lead so
often puts to sleep.

the help of dance to get ideas moving, Dom Helder is thinking of asking the help of the circus! They know that clowns, by helping us laugh, have truths to tell us that only they can make us understand. And the acrobats, the magicians, the lion-tamers, ah! . . .

Where did you get the idea to be like this? . . . What got you helping the poor? . . . How old were you when you met Jesus so that you love him all this much? . . . How do I get to be a bishop of the poor? [These were questions asked by children.]

The Lord put men and women in my path who were living witnesses of God's existence and love. It all started with my parents. (My father, though, wasn't a practicing Catholic.) My mom and dad were willing to let me follow any idea the Lord might have for me, for my life. So I was very young when I first felt that I would like to be a priest. I never planned to be a bishop.

As for the poor—where I live it's easy to think of the poor. Actually, though, it was a French cardinal, Cardinal Gerlier, who suggested to me one day, in the Lord's name, that I could probably do more to use the gifts that I had received in the service of the poor. When you let the Lord launch you, you have to be ready for anything, even for the unimaginable, even for being a bishop!

Aren't you ever discouraged? Where do you get the strength to speak with all this energy and freedom? Where do you get the courage to defend the poor? How do you manage to cross the terrible deserts of doubt and discouragement?

The Lord knows my weaknesses. God is my friend and protects me from the most terrible doubt: the doubt against faith in the divine existence and presence. Once we have the privilege and responsibility of believing with absolute certitude that the Lord is there, always, not only among us but actually within us, when we live and experience oneness in Christ, which we receive in baptism, we have the strength, the actual courage, of the Lord. With Christ we find our way through the deserts very well. We know that with him even deserts can be fertile.

2

YOUR PRAYER?

You haven't mentioned prayer. What place does it have in your life?
Can prayer help us?

Ah, prayer! It's there every instant of your life! God is
everywhere. Day and night we're plunged in the Lord. We
walk, we talk, we live, we're always within the Lord. And God
is within us. How beautiful it is to look at all of nature and to
converse—not with words, but only by thought—with the
Creator who is inside us!

This is incomparable strength—to know that we have the
Holy Spirit. What wealth it is to discover the seven gifts the
Spirit brings us all. We are so far from knowing how to use
them well! What wealth it is to become aware of the particular
gifts the Spirit has given to each of us, suited to each of us
individually!

And what a privilege it is to believe that we are one with
Christ! I like to say Cardinal Newman's beautiful prayer to
Christ:

Lord Jesus, conceal Thyself not within me thus! Look
Thou through my eyes, hear by my ears, speak by my

God is within us. How beautiful it is to
look at all of nature and to converse—not
with words, but only by thought—with the
Creator who is inside us!

mouth, walk with my feet! Lord, may my poor human presence recall, at least distantly, Thy divine presence!

These truths, lived by the Lord's grace, prepare us for Holy Mass, the pinnacle of each day. We have the responsibility and joy of knowing that the true celebrant of the Mass is always Christ. The Mass is the continuation of Calvary. The only difference is that today Christ can no longer die. But he, the well-beloved Son, at Mass, just as on Calvary, adores the Father, thanks God, asks forgiveness on our behalf, and offers prayers in the name of all human creatures of all places and all times, of all races, all colors, all religions.

The Mass is so high, so broad, so deep, that it covers the whole day. Try to discover how everything becomes offertory, how everything becomes consecration, how everything becomes communion!

It's easy to give Mary her whole, rightful place in our life. She is a creature, but a creature chosen by God to be the mother of her divine Son and our mother. And the saints? They're not gods, not in the least. But they are models for us—I often think of Francis of Assisi or Vincent de Paul—and they pray for us to Christ, our one savior and our brother!

Now all of this is prayer lived without effort, without sacrifice, prayer lived in joy. This is all a help, a force, that can't be measured. All of this unites us to creation, to creatures, and especially to other human beings. How could we forget that Christ has joined the first and second commandments together forever—love for God and love for human beings—as one great love?

With prayer and with the help of God's grace, our heart expands ever more and more toward the dimensions of the heart of Christ.

3

YOUR HOPE?

You see so much misery, so many injustices, and so little effort being made to combat them. How can you still be so smiling, joyous, optimistic?

I shall try to tell you. You remember that God was willing to let Sodom live, have a future, have salvation, if Abraham could find there not fifty, not forty, not thirty, but only ten just persons. This is the same God who looks at the world today, just as always. Suffering, injustice, and selfishness offend God. But God knows the weaknesses and strengths of all creatures. God respects them and loves them. God sent the Son among them, and left them the Spirit. God knows that there are far more than ten just persons! How could I not share the trust that God places in God's daughters and sons, my sisters and brothers?

In my country and everywhere I go it is true that I encounter misery, misfortune, violence, hate. But it is also true that I encounter numberless crowds of men and women, young people of all ages, who refuse to accept this situation, who thirst for justice and peace, who are ready for anything when it comes to building a world where people can breathe, a world of brothers and sisters. This gives me enormous courage.

In our base communities, in our sharing
groups, when our people read, hear, and meditate on the Scriptures, often the clearest word,
the strongest, the most evidently evangelical
word, comes from the poorest of the poor, from
the least important persons. . .

The poorest people you meet, the ones to whom you witness—do they share your hope? Even if they are in jail? Even if they are tortured?

They don't share my hope; I share theirs. Over my life I have learned a great deal from the ones who are called the poor but who are rich in the Spirit of the Lord. In our base communities, in our sharing groups, when our people read, hear, and meditate on the Scriptures, often the clearest word, the strongest, the most evidently evangelical word, comes from the poorest of the poor, from the least important persons, from those who cannot even read. I think of how Jesus thanked his Father for having revealed God's love to the small and lowly and not to the educated and the wise.

When you visit jails and prisons, when you speak with men and women who have undergone the most atrocious tortures— just listening to them gives you a fantastic store of courage and hope.

The Lord identifies with these men and women—prisoners, foreigners, the sick, victims of all kinds of oppression—and through them Christ reveals to us and lets us share his infinite trust in God's love.

4

YOUR GOD?

This God in whom you trust—is that the same God who made this world? Many of us have difficulty believing that. It's hard to follow you. There are those who say that the world is the way it is because human beings are sinners. Isn't injustice, which is the result of sin, willed by God? Why has God created human beings to be sinful? Why, how, does God allow injustice and suffering? How can anyone see God in a world like this where people are crushed and humiliated, where they lose the people they love most? Dom Helder, give us reasons to believe that God exists!

God, who is infinite wisdom, knew very well, in deciding to create something outside the Godhead—which is supreme perfection—that creation would be finite, limited, imperfect. But God did create. And creation will forever be the great testimonial to God's audacity, to God's humility!

But the supreme daring, the supreme humility of the Creator was to take one creature, the human creature, and make that creature a co-creator, sharing in the divine intelligence and power, with the responsibility of subduing nature and finishing creation.

It is a pity that human beings have made use of their divine gifts—the intelligence and freedom—to wound the two great

But the supreme daring, the supreme humility
of the Creator was to take one creature, the
human creature, and make that creature a
co-creator, sharing in the divine intelligence
and power, with the responsibility of subduing nature and finishing creation.

commandments, love of God and love of neighbor. But be careful! God didn't create sinners. He created human beings, and they commit sins.

Why doesn't God prevent human beings from committing sin? God's ways are not as our ways. We grant someone liberty on condition that our will will be completely respected! Fortunately, God knows us better than we know ourselves. God knows that there is a great deal more weakness than malice in this world.

The Bible, the word of the Lord, teaches us to say, "Lord, you are just! And so you will treat us mercifully!" God knows that we do not submit to divine justice, but that we hope for God's goodness and mercy.

As for the calamities that fall upon the earth, that crush and kill thousands and thousands of people, God gives us the intelligence we need to overcome them. There remains the other terrible calamity: selfishness, which leads us to a pessimistic appraisal of creation by the Father, redemption by the Son, and sanctification by the Holy Spirit. Selfishness, which is not the monopoly of any individual, leads to such absurdities that one day, clearly, human beings will grasp the need to be delivered from it.

But disease, accidents, handicaps, bereavement—all of these "natural" sufferings, all of these misfortunes that fall upon the innocent— are they too somehow the result of our will and freedom?

Misfortune, innocent suffering—I cherish what Cardinal Veuillot said after he had come to know suffering firsthand: he charged his priests never to speak of it without knowing it.

Personally, I like meeting up with mysteries. When I come to depart this life for eternity, I should like to carry with me a few questions to ask, some hypotheses to verify. Of course the great mysteries will always be beyond us, despite all God's efforts to make us understand.

The Lord encountered suffering. He wept. He took pity on the crowds. He tried to heal, to feed, to console. He even gave a child who had died back to her parents. When he was in agony himself, he asked for mercy. He never said that suffering was good or necessary or just. He never gave edifying sermons.

Our God was willing to create a universe. In doing so, God had to be willing to take the blame for having given life to what is imperfect. But God has given men and women the power and responsibility not to resign themselves to the misfortune and suffering of the innocent, but to fight it. This is our task.

Don't you think that we have made God in our image rather than vice versa?

I believe it was the great Voltaire who said something like, "God created man in his image, and man made him wish he hadn't." Actually we have often distorted God, making God the answer to our ignorance, compensation for our impotence, consolation for our anguish. The powers that be have made use of God to justify their domination, their ambitions. Today we are more careful about these pitfalls. Nonbelievers, by asking us questions like yours, have helped us to a greater respect for God.

5

DO WE BELIEVE IN ORDER TO HOPE?

Why must you Christians always link your humanitarian actions to a God? Don't you believe that belief in the human being is enough? Is it really necessary that God exist, is it really indispensable to be a Christian to combat injustice? Don't you think that one can achieve the same goals without any reference to God? You speak a great deal to Christians, to believers. Do you think nonbelievers have no contribution to make to the building up of justice and peace, or that Christians don't have to cooperate with them? Dom Helder, is it really necessary to believe as you do in order to have your hope and make your commitment?

My friends! Forgive me if I have given the impression that only believers and Christians can work for a better world. Ah, not at all!

When I look around myself, it's so clear that a great number of people who call themselves believers have no hope for peace, for justice, and for the happiness of all here on this earth and that many who do not know God or believe in God are involved in battles to the point of risking their lives.

In my youth I was taught that there were not only Christians

Sharing hope does not mean sharing faith. Those who do not believe have one thing in common with those who believe—namely, that the Lord believes in them. Of course they can, and should, work together!

by baptism, communion, the profession of faith, the celebration of the sacraments, and the observance of the commandments of the church, but also men and women who live the second commandment—''You shall love your neighbor as yourself''—without knowing that it is a commandment of God, or that it is the second, since they don't know the first. They were called ''Christians in act.'' The first one I knew, respected, and loved was my father.

Christians are sometimes reproached for not loving and serving human beings for themselves but for God. But if they are sincere, they are actually honoring the human being even if they don't mean to. Similarly, those who love and serve human beings for themselves, without any reference to God, if they are sincere, are actually honoring God even if they don't mean to.

Ah, what a surprise it will be when the Lord says to those who, without knowing or recognizing God, have lived the universal communion of brothers and sisters: ''Thank you for having received me, taken care of me, clothed me, fed me, defended me, done me justice. . . .'' What a surprise it will be when Christians, Catholics, see that they are not the only guests in the Father's house! The Father's heart is much larger than all of our parish registers, and the Spirit of God breathes everywhere, even where missionaries have not yet gotten off the boat!

So I say: no, sharing hope does not mean sharing faith. Believers know whence their hope comes and what their ultimate hope is. They have more responsibilities. Those who do not believe have one thing in common with those who believe—namely, that the Lord believes in them. Of course they can, and should, work together!

6

OUR RELIGION?

Doesn't that cheapen religion? You talk the way some of our young people do. They live the values of the gospel, but refuse to acknowledge a God at the heart of their lives. They believe in human beings but not in God. As a Christian I lose hope sometimes. What do you think about this?

One must let the young be young. They are on the road to the future. They will make discoveries. Many will find new ways of being Christian. We should like them to reproduce our own experiences. But have no fear—they will receive from us the best of what we have been. Be more attentive to what they proclaim. God loves the young. Jesus compared the kingdom to a tiny lost seed! And never forget: believing in the human being is not a mistake or a sin. God, too, believes in the human being!

There are young people who believe in God and who are even involved in Catholic action movements, but who don't practice their religion. We're uneasy. If they don't go to church anymore, if they don't hear the word of the gospel, how will they be able to hold up under pressure? What can we do as parents?

I understand your question. But I should like to make a suggestion. Ask your own children this question some day—not as a reproach or a challenge, but as a real question. It's natural for parents whose children have stopped eating at the family table to worry about how they will be able to restore and maintain their strength. They may not tell you what you can do about it. But they will surely tell you something you can understand. Then and only then you will know whether you have something to worry about. And you shall have to tell them why. If you are honest with them, as they will have been with you, you shall be able to continue your journey together, confidently and trustingly, along the unforeseeable pathways of the Lord. That is my suggestion.

I'm a nun. But I wouldn't care to deal with young people, because I wouldn't know how to talk to them about religion.

The young aren't actually trying all that hard to get you to talk to them about religion. But you can be sure that they look and listen and that they have a huge respect for those who lead a truly Christian life. Sister, think of all the known and unknown Mother Teresas! Think of the religious education being carried on joyously in prayer, in the service of human beings, in the service of the poor! The young have antennae. They know how to catch the signals of passionate, exciting love for God.

Are you aware of the ongoing drop in the practice of religion in France? What do you think about it?

Why always talk about the ''practice of religion'' instead of the ''practice of the gospel,'' the practice of love and courage, the practice of the service of others? It may be that this latter practice is not being abandoned. Maybe what is happening is just the opposite. Everywhere I go, including right here in France, I see something at work and I'm optimistic. If, as you say, the young go to church less, perhaps it is because they don't find the gospel and life united closely enough there. Then that is the Christian communities' problem: to join the practice of the gospel and the practice of religion so closely together that they become one and the same thing, as they were on Holy Thursday evening.

Why after two thousand years of Christianity is France less believing than Latin America? I've read that the countries that suffer from hunger are more believing because they hope for a better life hereafter. Do you think that the race for creature comforts and need-satisfaction withdraws industrial societies from the faith?

I can't think that the happiness of a father or mother is the unhappiness of their children. This would be an insult to God.

It is true that the poor populations of the third world and Latin America are very religious. But they are religious now not so much in order to win the happiness promised them in heaven after death through resignation to a hell on earth. Now it is more often because they recognize that Christ is among them to call them and help them share in the work of finishing creation, the work of the liberation of the world.

It isn't material progress that takes people away from the faith. It's the progress of selfishness. I know it's easier to be selfish when we're rich and satisfied than when we're poor and in need. You can see this in Latin America too. The Lord has warned us. God hasn't told us not to improve life on earth. God has asked us not to crush or forget the Lord along the way. God has reminded us that the Lord is the poor one, the one who doesn't count.

It isn't the progress of science, technology, and the economy

We should always pray and be converted, but we always do this by uniting ourselves to the Lord as the Lord appears in the faces of those in need. This is what Jesus himself told us.

that we should be afraid of when it comes to the future of faith but the progress of selfishness and injustice.

Even in industrial societies, faith has a future because there is, and always will be, a future for more justice and a greater communion of brothers and sisters. The Lord is there among you, the prisoners, the jobless, the foreigners, the ones you call the "fourth world." The Lord is at your door with the billions of poor of the third world. The Lord waits and hopes. Why would you be more deaf to God's call than your sisters and brothers of Latin America? Only because you are wealthier? No!

What do you think of the evolution of the church today? Isn't it a mistake to tune in too much to the world's wavelength, when the church ought to be firm, strict, and fervent in prayer and penance, with a deep respect for God?

It's hard to speak of the evolution of the church in a general way. Is it the same in France, in Poland, in Brazil, in Africa, in Asia? The Council has given everybody a big push. The Christian communities live this push, this thrust, in their own way, right where they are, with their responsibilities. Still, I feel that the church as a whole is moving toward a greater fidelity to the Lord's gospel.

We speak of the church and the world as if there ought to be a wall or a ditch between them. No, the church is in the world! It has never been on another planet, not even when it thought it was out of this world—or above it. The church is a way of living the life, the sufferings, and the hopes of human beings in the Spirit of the Lord. Of course we should always pray and be converted, but we always do this by uniting ourselves to the Lord as the Lord appears in the faces of those in need. This is what Jesus himself told us.

7

YOUR BROTHER JOHN PAUL II

Don't you feel that your positions go against those of John Paul II as he expressed them on his trip to Central America? If you are the pope's brother, as he says you are, he ought to be a brother to you, too, and look at things a little more as you do! Why was he so unfeeling in Nicaragua? Why that harsh "Silencio!" during that unruly Mass in Managua? The pope's trip to Central America was painful to us. We didn't think we were seeing the Holy Father welcomed by the church of the poor. We thought that we were seeing a condemnation of popular structures. Can you help us understand? I have the impression that the liberation effort of the people of Nicaragua has not received the same support from the pope as has that of the Polish people. What do you think?

Let me tell you to begin with: yes, the pope is really my brother. I love his passion for God and people, for truth and justice. He has enormous courage. He encourages me to have courage. His is a real grace of God.

To be brothers and sisters in the Lord and in the church does not mean being exactly the same, identical twins. It means mutual assistance, in all trust, to accomplish the different tasks the Lord has entrusted to us. For the pope this means being Peter, the one who strengthens the faith of the church, the one who decides. For a bishop, like me, it means being Paul, who comes to Peter with the questions of the world and the church. And with John Paul II, as with Paul VI and John XXIII, this is really the way things go—in a brotherly way.

I was in Japan when the Holy Father made his trip to Latin America. Afterwards I often heard questions like yours, and not only in France.

I met the pope on one of his trips, when he came to Brazil. I always say that it was a blessing. It was a trip he made hand to hand, heart to heart, soul to soul with the bishops of the country and with the priests, religious, and Christian communities united to the bishops. We had gotten together and prepared very carefully. The Holy Father has understood our great problems very well. He has helped us build an ever more liberated and liberating church. It seems to me that the bishops and Christians of Guatemala, El Salvador, or Haiti would say the same thing.

But I have the impression that the stop in Nicaragua has not been understood as a blessing by everyone. It is as if the pope's passing had revealed and hardened certain oppositions and divisions in the church there, just as, for that matter, it manifested and reinforced its unity. And so it is not so much the pope's words that one might wonder about, but the different commitments on the part of bishops and Christians who expect contradictory messages from him!

You know the situation in Nicaragua. For some, the number one danger is the installation of a communist dictatorship under the protection of Cuba or Moscow. Behind the revolution they see totalitarian oppression. For others, the number one danger, calling for the mobilization of Christians, is the social injustice and misery that crush the poor, God's "favorites" according to the Bible. In the revolution they see a chance for justice.

Everyone wants the liberation of individuals and peoples but not all place their trust in the same means. And so the questions raised by the Holy Father's stop in Managua are natural. They oblige us to recall that it is difficult to analyze conditions and then choose the route to a truly liberative revolution. Christians are like any other citizens. They have no magic formula. They are searching. But why, instead of opposing each other and shutting each other out, could they not search together— and search together with all women and men of good will who also want to create a world that is more just, one in which we shall breathe more freely, a world that is more human and humane?

Couldn't you consider a trip to Nicaragua? You could offer the support that the pope was unable to give.

I only go to countries where I am invited and always with the agreement of my brother bishops.

Certain forms of involvement on the part of the priests in Latin America have been condemned. What do you think about it?

As I've said, my personal experience suggests to me that partisan politics is not a priest's job. A priest's commitment is to live with the people, work with them, help in their conscientization, promote human betterment, and foster the revelation of the image of God that is in every human being. The priest's commitment is to lend a voice to men and women who have no voice, while others toil to win for the people the right to be consulted, the right to speak.

Saint Paul in one of his letters borrowed the old Roman comparison of society with a body. It would be useless and foolish for any individual member or group, even the head, to seek to take over all of the functions and responsibilities of society as a body.

The Holy Father has sown seeds of hope,
renewed the reasons for living, gathered
the courage that had been scattered and
dispersed!

What a wonderful thing it is to find each member in his or her or their place, performing precisely the function with which that person or group has been charged! This applies to the church as well.

The laity is the church, just as the hierarchy is. When politics means concern for the common good and for human rights, the whole church is called to engage in it, to act. When politics means commitment to a party, the hierarchy should encourage those who fight for the existence of parties (without ever accepting a one-party system), should help the laity to examine programs and question leaders, invite them and train them to get involved. Within the church, lay people, who are just as much the church as the hierarchy is, have the special task of being attentive to the world's affairs.

I should like to know what effect the pope's trips have in countries living under a dictatorship. I get the idea that after he leaves there is more repression than before.

It is true that persons in power try to make use of the pope, for example, by appearing on television with him. But the people understand what the pope says. The dictatorship may think that it is stronger afterwards, and it may repress the people even more than before, but the Holy Father has sown seeds of hope, renewed the reasons for living, gathered the courage that had been scattered and dispersed!

8

IS THE CHURCH REALLY WITH YOU?

Aren't you the tree that hides the forest? Do you get any support from the other bishops and Christians of Latin America and Brazil? In many Latin American countries the hierarchy gives the impression of being on the best terms with dictatorships that oppress the poor. Is that only my impression? There are those who say that one way or another the church is always on the side of power. Your life and the lives of certain other persons prove that it doesn't have to be this way. But what can one answer? And what do you think of the forces that proclaim their Christianity loud and strong, but spend all of the rest of their time torturing and murdering people who are simply asking to live with freedom and dignity?

My friends, I may be about to surprise you. You wonder whether the church is with Dom Helder. But that isn't the question. The question is, is Dom Helder with the church?

I say yes, I hope, I wish, I love to be with the church. Without the church there would be no Dom Helder. I would be neither bishop, nor priest, nor even Christian. I would have neither the joy nor the responsibility of the faith. And how difficult that is for me to imagine!

You see that the church is not always as lovely and pure, as brave and sincere, as it ought to be, or even as it would like to be. In creating the church, the Lord has embraced human weakness. But in promising never to abandon it, he has given it a very special strength. And he has never abandoned it. This is the extraordinary thing: despite its errors and betrayals, the church always faithfully hands on the good news, which the Son of God has come to bring to his brothers and sisters. The Beatitudes have never ceased to be proclaimed. The Magnificat has never ceased to be sung.

I'm an old bishop, and I have enough confidence to ask you never to resign yourself to the weaknesses, the compromises, perhaps even the treachery of the church—nor ever to despair of the Spirit of the Lord, who never ceases to dwell in the church.

You wonder if Dom Helder might be the tree that hides the forest. We may be using different binoculars, you and I. Where you see a forest of dictators, generals, torturers, aggressors, who crush the human being in the name of Christian civilization, and of bishops, priests, or Christians in complicity with them or afraid of them, I see a forest of men and women, of young people of all ages, who will not accept, who refuse, an alienated, alienating religion, who give their lives for human liberation. They are the church too. There are always more of them, and they are more determined.

Dom Helder is only a little tree in this forest, by God's grace. No, you may rest assured—Dom Helder is not alone! Not in Brazil, not in Latin America, not in France, not in Rome, not anywhere. Just look around you!

The Latin American Bishops Conference seems to have been taken over by the conservative wing of the church. They even say that it has come under the thumb of Reagan and the multinationals. Can you tell us whether the Conference is still on the side of the liberation of the peoples of Latin America?

Despite its errors and betrayals, the church
always faithfully hands on the good news,
which the Son of God has come to bring to his
brothers and sisters. The Beatitudes have never
ceased to be proclaimed. The Magnificat has
never ceased to be sung.

CELAM [Comisión Episcopal Latino-americano, the Latin American Episcopal Council] is a young institution. Still it has seen several periods: its organization before the Council, its period of theological reflection and evangelical meditation between the Council and the Medellín Conference in 1968, and then a period of searching and hesitation about applying Medellín, to cite some examples.

You have to understand that in Latin America the church has enormous influence. Whenever it really decides, not just in declarations but in life, to become a church of the people and for the people, to serve Christ, who identifies with the poor and the oppressed, those in power suddenly are all surprised and uneasy. This may be subversion, they think. Maybe communism has infiltrated the church. Then there are always people on the lookout for "imprudence," or "naiveté," and who find the means to prevent it. But while all of this is going on the Holy Spirit is preparing us for whatever great deeds of daring may be necessary.

Liberation theology would seem to have run into some opposition today with the emphasis back on Christ as savior or redeemer rather than as liberator. Why all this fear of the word "liberation"?

You know, it's not so much the name that counts. It may be that certain people have not completely understood the meaning of the expression "theology of liberation." They have heard that it is "Marxist" or something like that. Others have correctly understood that it is a rediscovery of the revolutionary power of the love of God in the history of human beings, and this seems dangerous to them. And so a great debate rages around the theology of liberation.

But no one can deny that Christ wills that all Christians work for the liberation of all of their sisters and brothers. Human betterment—the struggle against the causes of injustice, the conquest of dignity—is the right reason for human beings to cooperate in achieving the salvation and redemption for which the Lord gave his life.

Why this obsession with communism? Doesn't the church see that capitalist society too is a source of injustice and exploitation?

One of the big differences is that communist societies frequently deny people their basic freedoms. They do not include any democratic counterbalance in their institutional functioning. You can't argue with power. Criticism is practically stifled. Is this not one of the great dangers of our times, to see democracies disappear, even if they are capitalistic and imperfect?   .

How do you explain that the church—that is, we Christians—have been so slow to become once more, at least in desire, the church of the poor?

The church has always been the church of the poor in desire, through its millions of saints, known and unknown. And often it has been so in fact. At times the Spirit of God has made use of the church's adversaries to oblige it to practice more poverty, as when it was forced to divest itself of the Papal States, or, in France, when it was delivered, in spite of itself, from the privileges of the Concordat. But it must always begin anew.

During the Council I thought I understood what the church of the poor was. But later, when I lost my own freedom of speech, my reputation, my very name, I understood that poverty is something altogether different from a wooden pectoral cross or a very simple residence. One is never ''done'' being converted to Christ present in the poor, never ''all finished'' understanding what John Chrysostom meant when he wrote, ''The poor are our teachers.''

Shouldn't the church reconsider its ambiguous position on private property?

I do not think that the church's position on this point is ambiguous. From the Fathers of the church to John Paul II, it is clear that Christians can never consider themselves ''owners,'' since they are only the ''managers'' of goods, as gifts or functions entrusted to them for the service of their brothers and sisters.

What about the Vatican billions? We Jocists [Jeunesse Ouvnère Chrétienne], working-class Catholic youth, don't understand it and we don't like it. But John Paul II believes in it. Don't you think that the pope should at least be more simple in the way he dresses and in choosing where he lives before he starts talking about people's misery? Is there any hope that the pope might one day be liberated from a temporal burden that is an aberration and that has nothing to do with the mission of Peter's successor?

You know, things are already a lot different from as recently as thirty years ago. Our popes have already liberated themselves from as much as they could—from the tiara, from the *sedia gestatona* or portable throne, from their royal funerals, and so on. John Paul II is no longer the ''prisoner of the Vatican.'' He travels. He visits the priests and parishes of his diocese. With the Council and the Synods, the Holy Father listens to the churches. The change is wonderful. And so we can well imagine, and even hope and expect, that things will be even more different tomorrow, that the church will find the courage and the means to be delivered from the trammels of money, and, for the pope, from the constraints of a head of state with quaint, medieval bodyguard, diplomats, protocol, and all the rest. I am confident that if we fail to find this courage and these means—after all, it won't be easy—God will once more find a way personally to snatch us out of the rut of history!

It is so hard to live amid all of these ambiguities where the church is concerned. Don't you despair of the church sometimes?

Not on your life! Not for a minute! I've told you: to despair of the church would be to despair of Christ! But to live in the church means always wishing it to be more faithful to the gospel. This is something that will have to be suffered for and striven for in each new generation.

9

WHAT ABOUT OUR OWN CHURCH?

*Here in France you find precious few bishops accused of communism!
That must mean something.*

Very simply, it seems to me that it's either because there
aren't any bishop-accusers in France or because they're
smarter than ours are.

*Could you tell us why you don't see the church here involved in
Catholic Action movements committed to struggling against misery
and social injustice? Why don't our priests here in France do more
direct, more concrete work, as I saw done in Rio? Why is it so
difficult here to get the church hierarchy to listen to us workaday
Christians, to us God-seekers, to us gropers-in-the-dark, here among
the abandoned elements of our population? We have activists fighting
against the robotization of factory workers, we have people organizing
committees to inform the public about nuclear affairs, we have
farmers forming unions to work toward a better world economic
organization. You don't see these people in church much, and the*

church doesn't give them much support. So, Dom Helder, where are
there any signs of hope for us in the things you're saying?

My friends, you will have to forgive me. Those are questions
I carry with me, in my heart, in my prayer—but they are
questions that I cannot answer. Every time I come to France I
see things that are quite different from the things you are telling
me. I understand that, in your country as in mine, there are
always reasons for thinking that things could be better. Why?
How? You shall have to speak of this among yourselves. You
shall have to search for an answer together.

How can your experiences in Brazil and Latin America help us here?

I often hear that young Latin America has lessons to teach its
old parent Europe. No, my friends, we all have need of one
another's help. When I come here I tell the story of the living
faith of my people, which I know, and that spurs you on. When
I go back home I tell the story of the living faith that I have
found among you, and that helps us, encourages us enormously. This is how it was in the first century of the church.
The apostles exchanged news of the "wonders accomplished
by God afar," and Christians "gave thanks to God."

Exchanging news is very important in the church. It's the
circulation of the blood. It's communion. We must inform one
another, stir one another up to be, or become, Christians.

What are these base communities of which you speak so often?

In the base church communities, the people, by reading the
Bible, become really aware that they are a people of God. They
are truly a people of little ones, of the most abandoned, of the
"poor of Yahweh": the farm people, the workers of the subur-

In the base church communities, the people, by
reading the Bible, become really aware that they
are a people of God. They come together, they
read, they hear, they share the word of God,
they discover that they are recognized and loved
by God. Little by little, together, they take their
life in hand and work to make it more human,
more worthy of a daughter or son of God.

ban slums. They come together, they read, they hear, they share the word of God, they discover that they are recognized and loved by God. Little by little, together, they take their life in hand and work to make it more human, more worthy of a daughter or son of God. It is a movement of biblical fecundity and vitality. Bishops, priests, and sisters participate, and they are not there to work *for* the people, but to feed on the word of God in order to live *with* the people.

Wouldn't there be a place for base communities over here?

I don't know whether people in France are like our people. But I'm told that in France, too, there are communities and that they are on the increase. A life of sisterly and brotherly Christian communion, a joint quest for a life lived according to the gospel, can take different forms, but it is certainly one of the great calls of our times.

How do you see the future of ministry and consequently of the role of the laity from the standpoint of the base communities?

The role, or rather the roles, of the laity are just getting under way. For a long time the laity was passive. With Catholic Action they received the right to "share" in the hierarchical apostolate. Just to share. Since the Council, we know that the laity aren't just "those who aren't priests." Tomorrow they will be the ones to take charge of the church communities, to carry to the world the leaven of the gospel. We are at a great beginning.

10

CAPITALISM OR COMMUNISM?

Just what is your position on communism?

Up to the present, communism has always started out as a machine to seize power in the name of the people, and then it has become a machine to preserve and extend power against the people. I have never put any hope in communism. But I don't think that communism is danger number one. The number one danger is misery and injustice, the despair of human beings in which the false hopes of communism sink roots.

Do you pray for Yuri Andropov?

Like all men, Yuri Andropov is my brother. We have the same father. He has grave responsibilities and certainly works under great difficulties. I pray that he may, once at least, allow himself to be touched by the look in a poor person's eyes. Through this glance the Lord will show him the path of true revolution, the revolution of love.

I don't think that communism is danger number one. The number one danger is misery and
injustice, the despair of human beings in which
the false hopes of communism sink roots.

If a communist country awarded you a peace prize, would you go there as readily as you went to Japan to receive a Buddhist prize?

No, because I've always said I would never go anywhere that I wasn't sure I'd be able to speak with love and with freedom and without having my words used for propaganda. There is only one country where I've been willing to be without freedom, and that is Brazil, because that is my country.

Can Christians seeking to change the world in the name of their faith and hope actually choose a path as radical as that of the Marxist-influenced revolutions?

I have a great deal of respect for those who in all good conscience make this choice. But I have to tell you frankly, that if it means the route staked out, directed, and protected by the great capitals of state communism, while I still respect it, I don't share it. It may mean breaking away from one slavery, but it means falling into another slavery. Still, there are many situations in which waging a battle for the human being side by side with communists can advance the cause of justice. So that's a different matter. We all know communists who are communists because that's their way of believing in men and women and serving their brothers and sisters, and not because they want to grab power so they can hand it over to Moscow, Peking, or Havana.

Can there be justice in communism?

Marx thought so. But his successors have not proved him correct.

You say that you have no need of Marxism, that the church is enough for you. But don't you think that the use of Marxism's economic theory could facilitate a better understanding of the mechanisms of exploitation from which you seek to free human beings?

You know, there is no human thought that doesn't contain at least a particle of truth, a particle of the Creator's thought. I love those who have the wisdom and humility to search the thought of others for what might help them understand the great human problems better and solve them better. I also love those who, without being Christians, listen to us when we say that the gospel reveals to us the true roots of misery, injustice, violence, and exploitation.

Do you think, as Father Gutiérrez does, that the only way out of the situation of misery and exploitation in Latin America is socialism?

The difficulty here is to be sure we're all talking about the same thing. Socialism has meant, and still means today, very different political and economic teachings and practices, from state Marxism, in all of its heartless purity, to a social democracy that is rather more democratic than socialistic. My thinking is that neither American-style capitalism nor Soviet-style communism can provide the poor with a future of justice, dignity, and freedom. So we must look for something else. And when we find it, if it is called socialism that won't bother me.

There is a third way that seems to have wedged its way in between capitalism and communism, with its own particular organization and means. You don't mention this. Could you tell us what you think about it?

I am neither an economist nor a politician. I have no organization or means to propose. I do see this, though, that all over the world, east and west, north and south, more and more people are rejecting both unbridled capitalism and totalitarian communism. Surely this must be true in France, too, on the left as on the right, as you say, and among Christians and non-Christians. They search, they try, in the unions, in the universities, in businesses, in political or other group movements. So all I can tell you is: find these people who are searching, who are trying. Join them, help them.

Aren't you taking on a terrible responsibility, raising people's hopes like this without offering them some means of attaining what they hope for?

It would be an even more terrible responsibility not to share the hope I receive each day from the Lord, from my people, from everyone I meet. What I have I give you [Acts 3:6]. Forgive me if I am unable to give you what I do not have: a knowledge of the means—which will be different in each situation—to transform hope into effective will. It seems to me that this is your responsibility, where you are, as it is mine in my diocese.

If the church recognizes its mistake in having collaborated with the right in the past, isn't it making the same mistake in taking its position on the left today?

When I tell my own story and draw lessons from it, I recognize the error of having been too closely tied to power. I don't mean just power on the right. Besides, in our country it's often difficult to tell the difference between right and left. The real difference is between more or less democracy and more or less oligarchy, authoritarianism, dictatorship. The governments with which the church in Brazil, and I myself, have been too closely connected have been of every shape and shade. My experience has taught me that if the church wishes to stay free for the gospel and free to hear and serve Christ among the poor, it must not be tied to any power, right or left.

You say communism isn't the number one danger. There are Christians willing to ally themselves with the communists to combat the anticommunist dictatorships. Don't you think that dictatorships that suspend civil liberties are at least better than communism, which crushes the freedoms of heart and soul?

To me, all dictatorships are horrible. We must fight them all. We only have to be careful not to escape the clutches of one only to fall into another.

11

SHOULD WE TURN OUR BACKS ON PROGRESS?

In your censure of capitalism, you say profit seeking leads to absurdi-
ties, to disorders that no one can control, with the poor peoples and the
poorer among the rich peoples paying the price. In our developed
societies, profit and growth go hand in hand. Renouncing growth
means renouncing progress. Ought we to renounce progress? Ought
we to return to an agricultural, craft, and more manageably human
economy, to a life of autarkeia, *as certain third-world elements*
insist?

If I speak in the name of God and the poor I cannot be
against progress. When I see how much the human mind has
already invented and manufactured to deliver women and men
from cold and hunger, from pain, sickness, and suffering, from
ignorance, from isolation, and so on, I have to say: we must go
on. There is still far too much hunger, pain, disease, ignorance, and solitude.

Human beings, God's co-creators, still have a great deal to
do to finish and perfect creation, the mission they have received from the Lord. They must still dream, always dream,
and work for the revelation of all of the wealth that is only

Let us never retreat from the challenges of progress. Let us not imagine that the earth was more beautiful, more just, more peaceful, more free before the invention of the laser, or electricity, or steam, or the printing press, or the wheel, or fire. Let us bear in mind that the only truly humane solutions to human problems lie along the road of progress.

waiting for women and men to put it to work before it will begin serving life and taking its place in the High Mass of creation: offertory, consecration, and communion. They must reveal all the riches of the universe, already known or as yet unknown, and not only that of our little earth. Ah, when I think of the energy of the stars! Perhaps this will be our next step.

No, my friends! Let us never retreat from the challenges of progress. Let us not imagine that the earth was more beautiful, more just, more peaceful, more free before the invention of the laser, or electricity, or steam, or the printing press, or the wheel, or fire. Let us bear in mind that the only truly humane solutions to human problems lie along the road of progress.

But I understand your questions. They echo the questions I am asked by millions of men and women who, in our country as in yours, are cut off from progress, and even, very often, become its victims.

And so I say to you: let us walk courageously, daringly, along the road of progress. But let us be careful not to crush anyone, not to leave anyone lying in the ditch. The progress we have to make first, then, may not be in our super-laboratories and super-factories. It may have to be made in our minds and hearts. What I mean is that it will have to be made in our appetite for and will to progress. Progress for what? For what kind of growth? For whose profit? There is no truly human progress without progress in social awareness, social conscience.

Don't the imbalances with which we are faced come from an evolution based on rapid industrialization to the detriment of agriculture?

Agriculture is industrialized, you know, even in our country. And it is true that if industrialization is ill-managed, this can create grave problems. This can kill people, kill families, crush peoples—for example, when the industrialization of agriculture occurs without respect for farmers, driving them from their land, or when great industrial projects get a country so deeply in debt that to pay its debts it must produce what sells in rich countries best instead of what feeds its people best. And so you see agricultural countries practically starving. It is not industrialization that is to blame, but the way people develop it.

Won't the development of research, or of robots, for example, possibly deepen the chasm between the rich countries and the others?

When I was in Japan I met one of the greatest robot inventors and engineers in the world. There is nothing he can't think of. I thought, God must be happy that there are co-creators like this among human beings. But I thought of my people in Recife, too, who obviously aren't thinking of how to get out of work—very often they can't get enough work to feed their families. So I had a prayer in my heart that God would let this Japanese robot-creator meet my people, and that that would give him the idea that the fantastic progress that he has in his head and hands should serve first of all to make the poor less poor, and not the rich more rich. I invited him to Recife.

You are always denouncing the multinational corporations. Could you explain just how they are dangerous—how they might make the poor even poorer?

Multinational corporations are companies for which human beings are worth only what they bring in. Like any other capitalist company, their law is the law of maximal profit. For them this law doesn't even have the brake or counterbalance of social responsibility. When the profits dry up here, they close down and go somewhere else. Decisions are made far from the company's real life with nothing in sight but anonymous reports, tables, and numbers. I often meet managers of factories that depend on the multinationals. They always tell me that they have neither the right nor the means to make the decisions that seem to them to be just and humane because they are not the actual employers. The employers live somewhere else. You don't even always know exactly who or where they are.

For multinational corporations the places that yield the most profit are obviously the ones where raw materials and labor are the cheapest. This will be mainly in the poor countries. But profit has no connection with the usefulness of the product for the country in which it is produced. In fact, there will be more profit if this product is not used on the spot, but sold in other countries, where purchasing power is greater. This profit is only reinvested in the country if there is no better place to invest it. The poor countries pay the price of this logic more often than they reap its benefits.

12

HOW CAN WE HELP THE THIRD WORLD?

Dom Helder, when in your talks you ask for justice and solidarity in the name of the third world, lots of questions are raised. Some are general, others more particular. For example, by what means do you think it would be possible to share the world's wealth more appropriately? What do you think of rich countries' aid to the third world? How can this aid escape reappropriation by the imperialisms of East and West? Is it true that aid in the form of foodstuffs retards the genuine development of the third world? What is the main cause of the domination of the South by the North—the ravaging of third-world raw materials and food resources, or the dumping of our manufactured products and food surpluses on the third world? What can be done so that products coming from the third world will be suitably compensated, remunerated? Isn't the stabilization of the price of raw materials a primary duty in justice? Can mini-projects for development centered in the developing country itself, as proposed by third-world groups, have any effect? In a word: can there be an effective aid policy for furthering third-world development?

Many are trying to find it. For thirty years the best minds in the world have been looking for it. They are trying to understand the reasons for underdevelopment or nondevelopment. Every time they think they have it, they see that they have to look further. We can help them look.

I thank you for asking questions that bespeak your conviction that there is something to be done. You know, there are still people who think that the reason there are poor and rich is that that's the way God wanted it, or because there are lazy or inept races. It's ridiculous!

And so it's thought that if underdevelopment doesn't come from God or from nature, maybe it comes from technology. There are peoples who have scientific and technological resources, and there are other peoples who do not. The solution is what they call technology transfer. But we see very quickly that it isn't easy to create factories, generating plants, roads, or TV stations where there aren't any. We see, too, that when we succeed, very often we stimulate not the development of the country, but bubbles of artificial, anarchical, and unbalanced development that, either along with the development or afterwards, aggravate the underdevelopment.

In order to be an opportunity and not an additional risk, technology transfer must be well prepared and planned, right with the people who will assimilate it. This means that the people really have to be taken into consideration, their needs, their aspirations, their heritage, their projects. What is *not* needed are the Pharaonic programs that the leaders of the people so often negotiate with the multinationals or with the great commercial states.

Might it be that the industrialized societies, with all their technologies, are not a good development model for the underdeveloped countries? Ought the latter perhaps be left to organize their development themselves in conformity with their own resources and at their own pace?

The road of self-development is a difficult one. It is long. It takes time. It takes courage—the courage not to give up or be disheartened by comparing oneself with others. It supposes an

There are still people who think that the reason
there are poor and rich is that that's the way
God wanted it, or because there are lazy or
inept races. It's ridiculous!

abstention from involvement in the great economic currents of the dominant market and that that market will respect this abstention. How many countries now have all this? For how many more will it be possible?

And so we keep looking, and suddenly we think that underdevelopment is mainly caused, and always aggravated, by the destabilization, dissolution, and destructuralization of traditional societies, by throwing them into imbalance, by the violence of the international traffic in products, money, and ideas. These countries no longer belong to themselves. They are dominated by the laws and whims of the market, which depend on the needs of others and on decisions made elsewhere.

To stay the catastrophe there must be a reorganization of relations among societies and nations, a reform of international trade structures. This has been the grand plan of development strategy for two decades. But we see how difficult it is—it is difficult to bring so many different political wills into accord.

My friends, when we look for an effective development policy, we discover that there is not just one, but many that shall all have to be managed simultaneously, and all of them are difficult. The important thing is to get ideas and wills moving faster than underdevelopment. We have to hurry!

What do you think of the tons of foodstuffs destroyed each year by the farmers in rich countries to prop up or increase prices?

I've heard farmers over here in France say remarkable things about this scandal. They accused no one. They could see that the cause is an absurd, irresponsible organization of the economy. They were trying to organize, to be less victimized by, and at the same time to be less the accomplices of, this criminal absurdity. Ah, they taught me a great deal!

Brazilian soya doesn't feed Brazilians, but French calves, chickens, dogs, and cats. Should we stop buying soya since its production for export means, as you say, the impoverishment of the Brazilian peasants? I'm a farmer. Simply in order to provide for my children properly—that and nothing else—I'm obliged to buy Brazilian soya. But I wouldn't want to do it if the situation is as you say. What are we to do? What do you expect of French and European farmers?

Ah, my friends, if all of a sudden my country could no longer find a market for the soya that it's gone to such expense to produce, it would be a terrible blow at home. And I know that if all of a sudden you had to refuse to buy soya to feed your animals, this would be a terrible blow for you. But I have to tell you, I love it that you ask these questions. They express a remarkable understanding of the great problems of my people, which are your great problems, too. But, as there are no simple or separate answers, these questions can only be the beginning of the beginning of the process of imagination and political will to change the system, change the structures of the international economic disorder. This is what we in our countries call "conscientization," consciousness-raising. That's the first step, and it's a necessary one, since unless you become aware, no real change is possible.

What should be the principal role of a group committed to the third world? Consciousness-raising? Development projects? Lobbying or political action at election time? Some think the only way to keep out of politics is to stick to charity. Even particular movements, even Christians, quarrel over this in France. What do you think?

I'm very familiar with these quarrels. We have them too, since we're the ones with the third-world problems. But I don't understand them. The work to be done is so immense that there's room for everyone, for every attitude, every ability, for information, assistance, reflection, political action, and even for prayer. The roads are many, but they all converge because they all turn their backs on indifference and selfishness. And also because everything has a political dimension—not a partisan political dimension necessarily, but a political dimension. A choice for solidarity with the third world automatically means a political analysis and a political choice.

Do you think that the groups in France interested in the third world ought to form a federation?

I thought they already had, the Catholic groups at any rate, in the CCFD [*Comité Catholique contre la Faim et pour le Développement*]. I always say that the most important thing for small activist groups of good will is not to melt into a single bloc with one name, one leader, and one program. No, the important thing is that each group, keeping its own specific identity, find a way to communicate with all the others, with a view to mutual encouragement and stimulation, concerted action, and mobilization for certain great, prioritized objectives that will have been decided upon together.

What do you think of foreign volunteers in the third world, working with the people there and sharing their lives?

We have with us in Brazil some admirable brothers and sisters, priests, nuns, and lay people. They are from France, the Netherlands, the United States. But they aren't foreigners. They're brothers and sisters.

It's true, you can help the third world by giving it your life, by going there to live and work. But it is even truer, always, that things will really change for us only when they change over here. France, Europe, the United States, also need volunteers to commit themselves and give their lives for change!

13

WHAT CAN WE DO HERE?

Yes, you were the first to tell us, a long time ago, that we should work for change in our countries, and you are still saying it. But could you explain it in more detail, and give us some examples? Can you indicate some directions for us to take today to start the revolution we need over here?

Here you are, listening to me and asking me questions. You should be listening to and questioning one another! Answers abound on every side—and much better answers than an old Brazilian bishop could think up!

I remember—and this will surely ring a bell with you—in Rennes, in Grand-Fougeray, in La Roche-sur-Yon, in Nantes, in Angers, in Poitiers, in Cholet, in Laval—everywhere I have gone, I have been introduced to a great variety of groups of men and women and even children who have not waited till a certain Dom Helder came around to find what could and should be done. Dom Helder didn't speak; Dom Helder listened, and learned, and was struck with admiration.

I had the impression that here and there it was actually the first time these groups had met one another or perhaps even known of one another. I also have the impression that not all of the groups with answers to your questions have always been around.

As for concrete examples—not only of what it is possible to do but also of what is already being done to change attitudes, hearts, minds, habits, relationships, lives—I have collected plenty of them on my trip. They are examples of work for justice and for peace accomplished without hatred and without violence but with intelligence, resolve, and perseverance. I have seen examples of work with the jobless, foreigners, those excluded from progress—the ones you call the fourth world. I have run into examples of active solidarity with families, schools, villages, workers, prisoners, from Latin America, Africa, and Asia. I have seen examples of information projects, consciousness-raising, and reflection.

Allow me to suggest that meetings of volunteers for change such as these be repeated and multiplied in all cities, in all dioceses or departments, and not only when Dom Helder is on his way. Let me suggest that there always be an address, a name to contact for those who want to do something for a world that will be more just, a world where we can breathe, a more human and humane world. They will thus be able to discover what others have already begun to do.

How can we get all excited about injustice at home when third-world injustice is so much more of an emergency?

Injustice is one and indivisible. Any attack against it any-where that forces it to retreat makes justice advance every-where. We must not forget that although misery and injustice are more unbearable in the third world, the greatest roots of evil are in the heart, the interests, and the practices of the rich countries, with the complicity of the rich in the poor coun-tries.

Injustice is one and indivisible. Any attack
against it anywhere that forces it to retreat
makes justice advance everywhere.

Which is more urgent: to conscientize the rich while continuing to be one of them and to live among them, or to live with the very poorest to help them develop?

Both are urgent, but both are not possible for everyone. Each one must recognize what the Lord has made him or her best at, most inclined to. Only individuals can answer this question, with the advice of those closest to them, and their answer will apply to themselves alone.

Might our lifestyle and consumerism in one way or another influence the current economic system? There's been a campaign here in France to get people to "eat less meat, that's why the third world's poor." Is this a solution?

Yes, so I've heard. I think this campaign is a good idea—not by way of providing a solution, but as a shock to sensitize people, to help them discover a serious problem. Afterwards, even if they understand that this isn't the solution, they've still got the question. They're looking, and they can no longer live and think as before.

I often hear a consumer society condemned in your countries, as if it were shameful to consume! Not at all! What is shameful and scandalous is waste. And absurdly, it's the market itself that encourages waste. It feeds greedily on the profits of useless overconsumption. Overconsumption not only wounds justice—it wounds good sense, intelligence, and sometimes even your health!

14

CAN PEOPLE REALLY HELP?

How can we help the peoples of foreign nations, when most often their problems are internal ones that we can't get at?

Among all peoples there are individuals who create problems, others who don't see the problems, and still others who do see them and want to solve them by real reforms, without hatred and without violence. You may not be able to get at the first, although it does happen that the pressure of international opinion, or of foreign partners, causes those who create problems to reflect. But you may be sure that you can help those in the last category. Alone they can do nothing. But with the support of an international corps of volunteers working for change, they can win courage, strength, opportunities.

I know of certain groups who helped third-world farmers do a better job of cultivating their land. When they left, all the good results disappeared. So what good was it? Just look at the French Revolution, the First World War, and decolonization: now we know that every revolution ends up in greater oppression. Can you really protect people against people? One way or another, humankind will always be sinners, and selfishness will always stop everything. I no longer

Being young means having reasons to live,
and the reasons the young have to live are
their reasons for hoping!

believe that human beings have any control over themselves in their craze for power, domination, and well-being. Even in families, even in the church, there is no peace. Nations are led by their interests, especially rich nations. They have no motivation to share anything with anyone. The actions of a few individuals will never be enough really to change things. So, Dom Helder: What hope is there? What good can it do to "get involved"?

How I should love to see the persons who asked these questions! I think they must be old people—not necessarily in age, but in heart and imagination! You can't be young and have doubts like that. Being young means having reasons to live, and the reasons the young have to live are their reasons for hoping!

To these persons, whom I imagine as pretty old and tired, I shall say: my friends, I'm sure you've suffered a great deal. You've been deceived, betrayed in your hopes. You're discouraged, bitter, skeptical. I can understand that. But have the patience to listen to an old man who shares the thousand, the ten thousand reasons for hope that today as ever the young offer us.

If our parents, our grandparents, our ancestors since the beginning of humanity had thought as you, you wouldn't be here to moan and despair. You'd still be looking for roots to live on and survive on between one tribal combat and another, or between one drought or flood and another. I'm not going to give you a history lesson. You know enough history to understand and recognize that the human condition has become richer from century to century thanks to the creative hope of successive generations. Then why think it's all over now? There are still many things going badly, as you observe. So this is scarcely the moment to stop getting involved—or therefore to stop hoping! Creative hope still has a huge future before it.

You see the sin that is ever in the human heart. But don't forget that Christ is there too in the human heart. With him, human beings can free themselves from the weight of their sin! The Lord's Spirit lives in the world. And so, my friends, if even before knowing Christ, Abraham had the wonderful, fertile daring to "hope against hope," how can we not have the trust to hope *with* the hope that the Father gives us through the Son and the Spirit?

15

WHAT GOOD IS IT . . . ?

When you don't know much about economics and only have a bit of hope, you're treated as naive. Isn't humanizing the economy something that takes an expert? Dom Helder, every time you answer a question you say, "It's complicated . . . it's complicated." This isn't very encouraging! If even those in charge, with their experts, are helpless to solve the problem of the poor, what can I do as an individual? I'm young, and I have the idea that getting involved in a movement is like being a drop of water in the ocean. The real decisions that can change things aren't up to me. And so . . . and so, Dom Helder, how can a person speak of solidarity, and live it, without utopianism—speak it and live it effectively?

Don't be afraid of utopia. I have a favorite saying: when you dream alone, it's only a dream, but when you dream together, it's real. A utopia shared . . . is the springboard of history.

And don't be afraid of being just a drop of water. Drops of water running together make brooks, rivers, oceans! You have to remember that at the source there really aren't all that many drops of water.

Above all, don't be afraid of being powerless before the all-powerful leaders and governments. They pass; the people abide. Finally a day has to come when the leaders find it in their interest to take account of the people's interests. Not in dictatorships, of course. This is why to get ideas moving it's always important to fight dictatorships.

Don't be afraid of being "naive" in comparison with the science of the scholars and the experts. What are experts and scholars but "naive" people who've studied and worked? Study and work have enabled them to develop and propound their theories. But you don't have to formulate theories to imagine and live justice and solidarity. With a Lech Walesa and a Mother Teresa, the naive the world over have models of inventive, generous, simple daring!

In Brazil I've lived a life of sharing with all the poor, in the simplest way imaginable. Now that I'm back in France, I don't find that simplicity. Isn't it easier to live poorly in a poor world than to live poorly in a rich, materialistic world? How can anyone live with the heart of a poor person in our money-based society?

In all the countries I visit I meet men and women, and even families, who ask these same questions. I've never found anyone who said it was easy. There is always a decision, a break to be made, a voluntary renunciation of the normal lifestyle, or the lifestyle considered normal by those living it. Some decide even to have their lodging, work, and money in common. For many, the involvement is more direct, more personal, as they share their time with prisoners, foreigners, young people or women in trouble, people out of work, and so on. I know it's difficult—I can tell you it's even difficult for a bishop in a poor country. But even if it were impossible for men and women, it wouldn't be impossible for God!

We applaud you in great numbers as you pass through. But how many of us tomorrow will be willing to drop to a thirty-five-hour work week with a salary cut in order to share the work?

God only knows. That's God's secret. But the number isn't the most important thing. I like to think of how the whole sky can be reflected in a single drop of water. . . .

How can we make ourselves available and act as you ask us to when our working and living conditions are deteriorating? I work in health care.

I'm sure you know how to be available, at least to share your smile with your patients. Do you remember the beautiful story in the gospel about the widow's mite?

There's a deep gulf between what you say and people's apathy and inertia. Over here the welfare mentality is turning more and more men and women away from taking responsibility for their lives. How could they take responsibility for the lives of others?

It's all very well and good to wonder about people who don't think and live the way we do. But it's still better to *be* a question oneself to these people, to get them to wonder whether it wouldn't be better and more just if they thought or lived in a different way.

My problem is the indifference, or even hostility, of Christians. How can we work effectively when we see ourselves rejected by a majority of practicing Christians, who accuse us of playing the socialist or communist game? You must know what this opposition is like. How do you overcome it?

I've learned that opposition helps us more than praise. It encourages humility. Without humility, you can't move a single step ahead along the pathways of the Lord. We have to accept contradiction as a vaccination against pride. We must

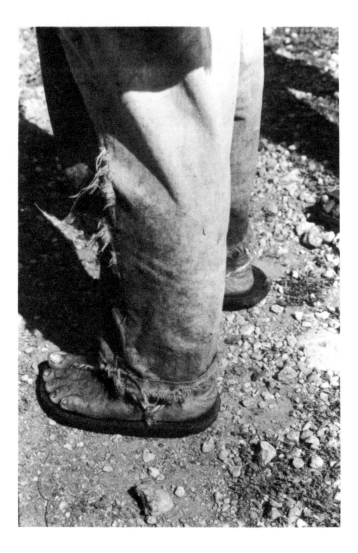

I've learned that opposition helps us more than praise. It encourages humility. Without humility, you can't move a single step ahead along the pathways of the Lord.

even welcome calumny, especially calumny we can't answer, as a way the Lord has of moving us ahead along the road of poverty.

In humility and poverty, all that remains is to place oneself at God's disposal and let God use the intelligence, wisdom, strength, and prudence that has been given us with the Spirit to convince our opponent and set things straight. And you know, the Lord manages some very surprising miracles!

Today, we listen to you, we understand you—and tomorrow at the offertory we drop in five or ten centimes or maybe a franc. Do you understand us? Do you condemn us? Do you forgive us? Me—I'm afraid. I stay in my cozy corner. My faith—well, maybe it'll help me some day. Help me!

I shall try. But it is not only for me to try to help you. Nor shall I be the main one to help you. The Lord is with you!

16

WHO, ME?

How can we send money to Brazil?

If it's money you're sending for a particular project, the best
thing to do is to ask those in charge of the project how you can
send them your contribution.

*Isn't giving money like being a godparent—it eases your conscience,
lets you think you're "practicing your religion"?*

Why shouldn't we want to have a good conscience? It's only
when we begin to suspect that we're not measuring up to all the
demands of our conscience that we have to take a step forward,
or several steps. But this is a suspicion that we can't accept
from others or apply to others. Conscience is always absolutely
personal.

*Is adopting a Brazilian child just another theft, or is it a helping
hand?*

In every country, even in rich countries, there are children
who are really abandoned, and not just because their parents

It's only when we begin to suspect that we're not measuring up to all the demands of our conscience that we have to take a step forward, or several steps.

or their mothers are driven to abandon them for lack of the wherewithal to rear them. Often these children if they had not been abandoned would have been condemned to the misery of being unloved. So for them adoption can be a helping hand.

What can a grandmother like me do?

Excuse me if I'm wrong, since I can't see you, but grandmothers today seem more like big sisters! When you tell me you're a grandmother, I think of my meeting in Rennes with the grandmothers and grandfathers (and some great-grandmothers and great-grandfathers!) of Peak Life. It was wonderful! The huge hall was full. I suddenly felt that I was in a crowd of people much younger than many of the young people who had found loads of worthwhile things to do. I'm sure they'd give you a better answer than I would.

17

YOUTH? ARE YOU SERIOUS?

What is it with these young people who couldn't care less no matter what you suggest to them? You always use the young as an example, but are you aware of the materialism that makes the young so passive? And what can we expect of so many youth who already bear the stigma of unemployment, and are shut out in that way? For some the only thing they can expect is unemployment, and their only interest is some sort of immediate satisfaction. And what do you think of the young who have lost hope in life and commit suicide?

Youth in despair is the most frightening thing I have ever heard of. In fact I have difficulty even imagining it. And you tell me it's right here, all around you! I tell you: don't accept it. Never! The worst thing to take from young persons is their reason for hoping. Have the courage to fight to get it back for them. And don't just fight: sacrifice, too, if necessary.

Don't you think that if children were taught to share and not be so selfish they could create a genuine new society?

This is exactly the responsibility of parents, grandparents, and schools too. But let's never forget that teaching children

Youth in despair is the most frightening thing I
have ever heard of. The worst thing to take
from young persons is their reason for hoping.
Have the courage to fight to get it back for
them. And don't just fight: sacrifice, too, if
necessary.

means first and foremost giving them an example. They have very sensitive antennae, which enable them to tune in to what's sincere and tune out what isn't.

What's your opinion of the young, and the less young, who go to the third world to learn what's going on?

If they really want to learn what's going on, it's better for them to be prepared, expected, welcomed, accompanied. Perhaps the best preparation is the encounter with the third world, or fourth world, here in the midst of the rich countries.

I'm ten years old. I'd like to share your peace message at school. Do you think I could do it? Are we too young to realize big human problems? What can kids over here do to help third-world kids?

Michael, Anne—I see your names here under your questions—you came to listen to me. Keep asking questions of your parents, your teachers, your priests. They're the ones who can help you learn to know and understand "big human problems" and then act. And I may as well tell you: *you*'ll be helping *them,* enormously, to stay alert to these problems because with your questions you'll be representing the third world to them.

I'm told that each year in France, as in other countries, there's a Third-World Day at school, right? What I would suggest to you, ask of you, would be to make this day something very important, something very strong, in your class, in your school.

I'm told too that the CCFD proposes precise and worthwhile activities to children each year. They call these Rainbow Projects. Why don't you too build a bridge of light and friendship like that between the worlds? Good luck, Anne, Michael, and the rest of you! Go for it!

18

CONCRETELY?

I just took my college entrance exams. What should I do next year? I'm a senior. I have to decide what to do. I'd like to go into training somehow to help third-world countries. Can you give me any ideas or advice? . . . I'm a university student. How could I help the weak, the third-world people, with my business major? I really need your answer. Otherwise it'll be hard to see any good at all in what I'm doing.

I'm asked questions like yours very often—questions that call for precise, urgent answers that, you see, I just can't give. Studies are different in every country, and sometimes in some countries they change from year to year. I'm sure there are qualified individuals here who not only can understand your aspirations but who know your talents and abilities and can give you advice.

But I'm going to keep your questions. They prove that here in France as everywhere young persons hunger and thirst for something besides a ''career.'' And I'll tell you something: there are lots more of you than you think. If you could get acquainted, get together, encourage one another, I guarantee you you'd no longer have any doubt about your strength. Nor would anyone else!

I don't look for ships or planes coming to us
with generous volunteers. I wait for the never-
ending, ever-increasing good news that men,
women, and youth believe, hope, and toil as we
for a better world.

I'm going to suggest an answer to you anyway. All jobs and professions are worthwhile if they're practiced not only with competence and honesty but also in the spirit of service. This is obvious in the business professions. But it's true too for just about any trade or profession.

I realize that not all jobs put you in direct contact with the third world. But I always say: going to the third world isn't the only way to move the world along the pathways of justice and peace toward a communion of brothers and sisters. When I'm back in Brazil and I look toward France and Europe, I don't look for ships or planes coming to us with generous volunteers. I wait for the never-ending, ever-increasing good news that men, women, and youth believe, hope, and toil as we for a better world. After all, your world is ours, your future is ours. Don't desert it!

19

SHALL WE LAY DOWN OUR ARMS?

You stir up Christians to do something for peace. But you certainly seem alone. What is the hierarchy doing? Why don't the pope and the church take a clear position against the escalation in nuclear stockpiling? Do you think the church denounces the arms race strongly enough? What are Christians in positions of responsibility doing?

No! I'm not the only one with the fine speeches and nice words! All of the modern popes, the Council, and a great number of bishops' conferences have issued denunciation after denunciation in no uncertain terms of the arms race and the dangers of nuclear war.

But we all know very well that it is not enough to denounce, to condemn. We have to propose solutions. The popes, the Council, the bishops' conferences, have done this: there can be no peace without respect for human rights, without justice among nations, without the creation of a world authority able to arbitrate conflicts, and so on. It's not their fault if their proposals get no better reception than their condemnations. Do Christians even know what these proposals are?

You ask what the church and the hierarchy do, what they

say. But I say, remember, the church isn't just the hierarchy. The church is the people, too, the laity. It's not just up to the hierarchy to supply the church with imagination and courage. It's lay people's job as well. It's all very fine to demand so much from the pope and the bishops. But the demand that really helps those responsible for the church is to demand that Christians agree and assert themselves.

If Christians always wait for the bishops to move before they get going themselves, and the bishops always wait for Christians, the church will never move ahead, it will never help the world move ahead along the pathways of peace!

What do you think of the American bishops' statement on nuclear arms and nuclear war?

I love this commitment on the part of our brothers in the United States as I would love a baby I'd practically seen born. I'm often invited to North America. In the parishes, the universities, among priests, sisters, young people of different religious denominations, year after year, I've felt questions welling up in the conscience of the churches, right up to the bishops. It was wonderful!

Now we have this great statement, this great declaration. I like the courage with which it contradicts the political analysis and choices of the current federal administration. But I also like the seriousness and lucidity of the bishops' research. They consulted a great number of experts. They tried to take account of technology, strategy, economics, sociology, and so on, and not just their generous feelings. They thought of all those who look down on or who fear the utopia of "great statements," of sermons on peace. Their positions and proposals are realistic. In this so complicated, so passion-ridden area of war and peace, realism is certainly a condition for a dimension of prophecy.

But I love the American bishops' letter for another reason: their method. This letter didn't surprise anyone. It wasn't sprung on people all of a sudden without their expecting it, without their being ready for it. No, over the course of a year the bishops produced several versions of their letter. Each version was published, advertised, and debated. Then when the actual letter finally came, the ground had been prepared, the community had been consulted. The word of authority was already a word shared!

Is a deterrent involving a threat to destroy cities a policy that Christians may support?

If I understand the Holy Father aright, if I understand my brother bishops aright in the countries where the problem is most acute, nobody is saying that the nuclear deterrent is morally supportable. After a great deal of discussion and much hesitation, what they are saying is that it can be, for the moment, morally tolerable. I think that "tolerable" is a great deal different from "supportable." You support something you believe in. You can only tolerate something you have reservations and regrets about—impatiently waiting to get rid of it as soon as possible.

This is why it is so important to understand and support John Paul II when he says that we must absolutely not believe that deterrence and the balance of terror can insure a stable peace or a genuine peace. Peace by deterrence is always a precarious peace. It is a peace that soon becomes corroded, its foundations undermined by the mortal illness of the arms race.

And so I ask you as your brother: listen to the pope; listen to the Council, which calls the blind destruction of civilian populations a crime; listen to the scholars consulted by the Pontifical Academy of Sciences, who foretell the catastrophic consequences of any nuclear war; listen to your good sense and your conscience! If you think you should tolerate deterrence for the moment, at least do not tolerate the idea that this horrible, perilous instant should become eternal! Do not let another moment go by before you set about stabilizing a peaceful future on foundations more intelligent, more sure, and more worthy of the human being than the threat of murder by millions and collective suicide!

Let a brother from the third world make one more observation to his sisters and brothers of the North. Look how the nuclear threat has protected you for forty years! The Third World War has not yet happened! But neither forget to look at how the great powers, under cover of their rockets, have fought each other for forty years, without interruption, without mercy, in the third world, through the intermediary of poor peoples! No, peace by nuclear deterrence is not peace for everyone!

Why don't you denounce, here on your visit to France, the manufacture and sale of armaments pursued by our administrations of left and right alike? How can we struggle concretely against the arms trade in a country and in cities where the arms industry flourishes so? What behavior do you advise to someone who works in a weapons factory? How do you imagine that the millions of French workers in the weapons industries could be put to work on something else? How could the twenty-five billion francs that our arms sales bring in be replaced? How could we defend France without an army and without weapons?

I always say: nowhere do I feel myself to be a stranger. I always try to be a brother among so many brothers and sisters. And it is as a brother that I have the confidence to say to you: the answers to the very serious, very important questions you are asking about the weapons you manufacture and that you sell are right in front of you. After all, you mustn't think that you're the only ones responsible! We too, in buying what you sell, take part in the ruinous, absurd, and dangerous arms trade. We too manufacture arms and sell them, and even sell them to France!

I know that your country, with ten percent of the world's arms market, is the third largest exporter of arms. I know too that the leaders of the Christian churches in France have publicly, clearly, and repeatedly denounced the perils of this power, and this wealth. It seems that you have not paid them a great deal of attention! Why? What good are the bishops' denunciations if Christians fail to hear them, fail to share them, fail to feel responsible themselves?

Many people over here work in the weapons industries. I doubt that they've chosen to do so. Who can really choose their work, especially when there is unemployment everywhere? We must not ask these people, who are doing what they can and what they should to feed their families, to solve problems that are beyond them. The solution does not lie in some persons quitting their jobs, heroically, although some feel bound in conscience to do so.

Armament workers, technologists, and engineers can, however, in company with their colleagues, their employers, political leaders, and experts, look for a way gradually to manufacture and sell something besides weapons without creating unemployment. We have to face the whole problem of the reconversion of the arms industries. The day will come when public opinion, employers, and political leaders will be mature enough for a different policy, a different strategy. There you have a wide-open, super-urgent project for someone who works in the weapons industry!

I remember during the Council some American unions came to Rome to beg the bishops not to come out completely against war because millions of workers would be thrown out of work. My friends, unemployment is a horrible thing. We must fight it. But it is impossible to think that only the war industries

As I've said—it's not only the rich countries that impoverish the poor countries with **the** arms trade. The poor countries impoverish themselves by believing that they have need of these arms for their prestige, their ambitions, or, in imitation of the great powers, for insuring their security by deterrence!

can offer employment. We can and should open the way to peace industries.

Don't you think that the arms race contributes to the impoverishment of the third world, and that instead of nice words about the third world, we would do better to fight our profitable arms sales to those countries?

As I've said—it's not only the rich countries that impoverish the poor countries with the arms trade. The poor countries impoverish themselves by believing that they have need of these arms for their prestige, their ambitions, or, in imitation of the great powers, for insuring their security by deterrence!

Here's the scandal: in 1982, all the nations of the world together spent over $700 billion for weapons and armaments— six percent of the world's wealth! The UN, the international experts, the popes, the churches, can never find words strong enough to denounce this waste that kills the poor by making them the prey of hunger and underdevelopment. This will never be acceptable.

I ask you: do these countries arm only because they have so much money that they can afford to waste it? No, these insane expenditures for guns, planes, and bombs have to be made at the expense of health, education, housing, and so on. Before there can be a better use of money there will have to be an end to the obsession with national security. This calls for a great deal more than protest against ever-growing military budgets. There will have to be work for disarmament—that is, for the political changes that will make it possible to move from confrontation to cooperation, from fear to trust.

What do you think of the pacifist movements and demonstrations? Are you manipulated by the Soviet Union?

I don't like the word "pacifism." It sounds too much like "passivism." And if it means peace at any price—even at the price of injustice or servitude, for oneself or others—then that of course will never do.

Where I go, in France too, I hear of movements and demonstrations that have no passivist intentions whatever. If I understand correctly, there are the people in Europe who judge it neither useful nor reasonable, but actually dangerous, to have more nuclear arms installed on their soil. They think that these new armaments will be more of an additional threat than an additional defense. If they have serious reasons to fear this, then they are right to try to convince others.

In the complicated game being played by the superpowers, it may well be that these movements are more embarrassing to the Pentagon than to the Kremlin. But this does not necessarily mean that these movements are being manipulated by the Soviet Union. We hear of similar movements in Eastern bloc countries, in East Germany, Hungary, even in Russia. To be sure they are forbidden and brutally stifled. If people there could express themselves as people can in the West—this would be impossible, of course, but if they could—Moscow would surely say that they were being manipulated by the United States. And yet obviously this would not necessarily be true.

There is always manipulation. But we may not allow ourselves to use our "realism" as a pretext for blinding ourselves to the profound aspirations of peoples in the West or in the East for an intelligent peace, founded no longer on more arms but more and more dialogue, freedom, and trust.

If war is a sin, what should our attitude be toward our armed forces, enlistment and draft, and conscientious objections?

I have enormous respect for the young people who in all conscience have the conviction that violence, even legal violence, is not the way to serve justice and peace. And I respect the states that permit these young people to be loyal to their conscience without punishing them for their convictions.

I always ask those who in conscience refuse military service, not to sit back and take it easy just because they're officially left alone. My friends, the violence you reject won't disappear or diminish simply because you've chosen not to participate in it! You can't rest on your laurels! You can't wash your hands of violence. If you think violence is an evil, you should also believe that only nonviolence can stop it. You should give nonviolence a push. So give the energy you're not spending in the army to nonviolence and action as a means of resolving conflicts and furthering justice!

You know, you won't solve the problems of superfluous weaponry and armed violence simply by increasing the number of conscientious objectors. You shall have to invent, experiment with, and call attention to means other than weaponry to insure peace in justice and freedom!

What would the Soviet Union do if the United States and Western Europe disarmed unilaterally? Isn't it naive to opt for disarmament when a superpower's one aim is to propagate its ideology? The experiment could result in a cruel disappointment! Seriously, then, can disarmament be unilateral? And isn't total disarmament utopian?

To begin with, at least we mustn't say that because disarmament is difficult and fraught with risk we shouldn't even think about it, much less work for it. No, disarmament is not optional! The thing is not impossible! It's the condition for humanity's survival!

To be sure, universal disarmament is the final objective. The question is what the first step should be to approach this final objective.

There are negotiations in progress between the superpowers, especially in Geneva. It's hard to place a great deal of trust in these negotiations. While the great powers engage in their discussions and from time to time come to agreements that slow the arms race—merely slow it down—the laboratories, factories, and the military are working to perfect a new generation of arms to negotiate about ten years from now.

So I understand and respect those who have the courage to explore other routes and to propose, not total unilateral disarmament, but initiatives that cut through the spiral of mistrust—especially if, at the same time that they take the first step toward disarmament, they install other systems of defense that don't require weaponry.

After all, human rights, freedom, and democracy obviously have to be defended. And so we must develop research everywhere on the power of nonviolence as a means for the defense of human communities, even against armed might. The disarmament we need isn't passive resignation to aggression and oppression: it's the invention of another defense.

20

DOES NONVIOLENCE WORK?

Do you know of cases where nonviolence has succeeded?

The history we learn in books and newspapers is a history of wars, battles, and violent revolutions. These media ought also to tell the story of the peoples who have resisted oppression without violence. There's more of this than people think.

In the nineteenth century the Hungarian people obtained a Statute of Autonomy in the Austrian Empire as a result of a campaign of civil disobedience and tax resistance. At the turn of the century the Finnish people resisted Russification through their organized disobedience to the Czar's orders. In 1920 the Germans foiled a military coup by means of a general strike and total refusal to obey the orders of an illegal authority. During the Second World War the Danes, by their collective behavior, prevented the implementation of the SS guards' plan to round up all the Jews. In California César Chávez led a long nonviolent struggle by migrant workers for the recognition of their right to unionize. Here in France we have the Larzac peasants, in the United States we can cite Martin Luther King, Jr., and in India, Gandhi. Today all have their eyes on Poland, Chile, and Pakistan.

Yes, there are cases in which nonviolence has succeeded, and there will be more and more of them because more and more people believe that true liberation comes of combats waged without hatred and without violence.

Are there rules for nonviolence? What are they?

The main rule, of course, is to absolutely refuse to commit any violence on persons' lives or dignity. But there is what we might call a strategy of nonviolent action. This strategy, of course, is adaptable, depending on the nature of the conflict and the forces against which the combat is to be waged. Generally speaking, the strategy of nonviolent action aims to cause the foundations of unjust power to collapse. Oppressive, repressive power rests on resignation, collaboration, and obedience on the part of the people. Nonviolence tries to organize noncollaboration and disobedience by as many people as possible. No power can last long, even by force of arms, against a whole population that refuses to obey it and recognizes another power instead. The strategy also includes a tireless dialogue with half-hearted agents of the unjust power to try to get them to rally to the cause of justice.

Those involved in genuine movements for nonviolent action study conditions of effectiveness—what works in which circumstances. Then they try to apply their findings. We need entire states, whole peoples, studying the conditions of effective nonviolence!

Are you for nonviolence on moral principles or merely for reasons of strategic effectiveness?

I know a great number of people who put more trust in arms than in active nonviolence in the struggle against injustice and oppression. I respect them when they make this choice in good conscience. With due respect for them I say that this is not my choice. In the name of the gospel, I prefer to be killed a thousand times than to kill someone else. I know that today you can't beat the arms manufacturers or their petty allies by force of arms. I also know that if you do succeed you'll have to preserve your victory by force of arms, and so it will not be a true victory, either for peace or for freedom.

Many individuals choose nonviolence for moral reasons, or even, very often, for religious reasons. They seek to resolve the everlasting question: how to act for justice, freedom, and peace without making use of means that, even if they appear effective at the outset, carry with them the seeds of death for justice, freedom, and peace. Many Christians wish to be faithful to the Sermon on the Mount and the example of Christ.

Many persons have chosen or choose nonviolence only because when they have no weapons this is the only possible way to liberate themselves, the only effective way. In his great struggle to liberate India, Gandhi recognized that if he waited till everyone had become morally convinced of the need for nonviolence, he would not get very far.

And so I say that we mustn't set morality and effectiveness in opposition here. A nonviolence unconcerned with taking action to make history would still be passivism, however disguised by great principles and noble feelings!

There are countries where the only response to dialogue is repression. How can the poor struggle for their dignity without yielding to violence? In Nicaragua yesterday as in Afghanistan today is there any other road to liberation than violence? Was there any other way of stopping or demolishing Nazism but violence?

As I've already said, I pass no judgment on those who, in a situation of horrible oppression, think that for them and their sisters and brothers the risks of nonviolence are greater than the risks of violence. One cannot pass judgment on choices made in good conscience.

But I say too: one ought always to go as far as possible along the lines of nonviolence. And one can often go much further than appears possible. We mustn't begin by setting limits to the effectiveness of a nonviolent action that has not even been thought of yet or tried out.

We sometimes hear that there are victims on the nonviolent side and that that proves that nonviolence has failed, that it is powerless! Not on your life! True, nonviolence refuses to create victims on the other side, but it is willing to have them in its ranks! The difficulty is in planning, preparing, and staging a nonviolent action thoroughly enough and seriously enough that the people don't abandon it after the first clash. There is no victory over oppression and the structures of injustice without sacrifices. Sacrifices accepted in nonviolence are a better preparation for the future and for reconciliation than sacrifices imposed by violence.

In order for active nonviolence to change the world, everybody will have to get involved. Is there any international orchestration of efforts?

I have already participated in three international gatherings of movements working for justice and for peace through active nonviolence: in Driebergen (the Netherlands), Derry (Ireland), and Nassogne (Belgium). In these gatherings you can see that nonviolence is becoming a force to be reckoned with. The difficulty lies in going beyond gatherings and meetings to real orchestration and then to the genuine mobilization of all of the groups toward two or three great human problems—with each group maintaining its own objectives, its leaders, and its specific name. But even this difficulty will be overcome one day!

Surely it would be wonderful, it would be irresistible, if

The aim of nonviolence is to force even a violent enemy to yield. This demands imagination, courage, and a great deal of solidarity. But it also means that you don't wait until your adversary has been converted to nonviolence! This is why nonviolence is something for today, not for tomorrow!

everyone engaged in active nonviolence! But our responsibility is to act in the world as it is—that is, without waiting for everyone to become aware of the necessity and possibility of nonviolence. Otherwise nothing will be done.

Don't forget, the aim of nonviolence is to force even a violent enemy to yield. This demands imagination, courage, and a great deal of solidarity. But it also means that you don't wait until your adversary has been converted to nonviolence! This is why nonviolence is something for today, not for tomorrow!

CONCLUSION

The editors at La Vie *asked Dom Helder a final question:*

Dom Helder, that was the last question from those who came to see and hear you in western France. But perhaps you have not said your last word. Might you have anything else to say to those who have questioned you and listened to you?

Yes. If your patience will permit, I shall add a few considerations at the risk of venturing into futurology.

In the area of economics, changes that seemed impossible dreams yesterday are already perceptible in reality, within arm's reach. Let me explain.

Large multinational companies have encouraged underdeveloped countries to undertake huge, Pharaonic projects of no use to the peoples of these countries and necessitating incredible international bank loans. And of course these loans are made with interest. The upshot of these loans has been not profit, but insolvency.

The International Monetary Fund, intended to aid underdeveloped countries, has been sucked into the game of the great financiers. In order to create the necessary conditions for the repayment of these loans, it imposes economic measures that provoke still more terrible unemployment and a still more brutal crushing of the masses, who already live in subhuman conditions.

And so I say: if a few third-world countries—like Brazil,

In our little galaxy, around our little sun that
seems so enormous to us, our Earth is but a
grain of dust. But it will always have the glory
and the responsibility of having been chosen for
the incarnation of the Son of God.

Mexico, or Argentina—could establish and negotiate more human and more secure conditions for repaying of their loans, they will be followed by ten, twelve, fifteen other countries that are in even greater difficulties.

It's obvious that the large multinationals and the international banks, whose ideology is based solely on profit, will find it in their interests to foster a more humane economic and financial system. They know that otherwise not only will there be no repayment, but there will be an explosion.

In the area of the arms race: I fear that humanity will not come to its senses until it has experienced, through a disaster a thousand times worse than those of Hiroshima and Nagasaki, the terrible capability of destroying life on the whole earth.

In the area of technological progress: in these modern times, the world has already seen two industrial revolutions and it is beginning to see a third. When steam engines appeared on the scene, people had the idea that they would bring happiness with them. Very quickly the truth appeared: the poor were crushed even more than before. Then electricity, and even greater hopes were raised. The poor continued to be crushed.

Now we have the fully automated assembly line, we have robots. This is the new challenge, a serious and decisive one: we must bring it about that robotization not be just for the profit of a little group of the ever richer while the huge majority are crushed even more than before. How might we bring this about?

In the area of the race for space: we're still in the prehistoric stages. But we can already dream of taming and harnessing the great forces of nature. With our petty little earthly energy sources, we cannot go much beyond the moon—unless we want to go into hibernation and wake up four or five generations from now. It's true that Einstein predicted that when human beings could fly at the speed of light their bodies would be volatilized! But it seems to me that when that day arrives, human beings, who share in the divine intelligence and in

God's creative power, will be well able to keep themselves alive!

In our little galaxy, around our little sun that seems so enormous to us, our Earth is but a grain of dust. But it will always have the glory and the responsibility of having been chosen for the incarnation of the Son of God.

I think that we honor the Lord's intelligence and creative imagination insufficiently if we think that God has created billions of stars, millions of times larger than earth, only to twinkle far off and be our joy in the magic of the night or only for the pleasure of creating the most monumental ballet. Surely the Lord has sown life throughout these worlds of worlds— intelligent, free life, on our own level, below it, and above it.

When the real space landings have begun, here and there men and women will at last be able to understand their little- ness and the greedy, cheap use that they have so often made of the gift of divine life, intelligence, and freedom in which they have been invited to share. When the real landings start, women and men will at last be able to measure how infinitely greater, how much more generous, how much better the Lord is than they have ever been able to imagine!

You young people—young in body and soul or young at heart, young because you keep your reasons to live—I offer you this beginning of a beginning of a meditation on the world.

Go further, infinitely further!
We shall never go too far!